WITHDRAWN

Murray, Julie.
Tennessee

1/07

Tennessee

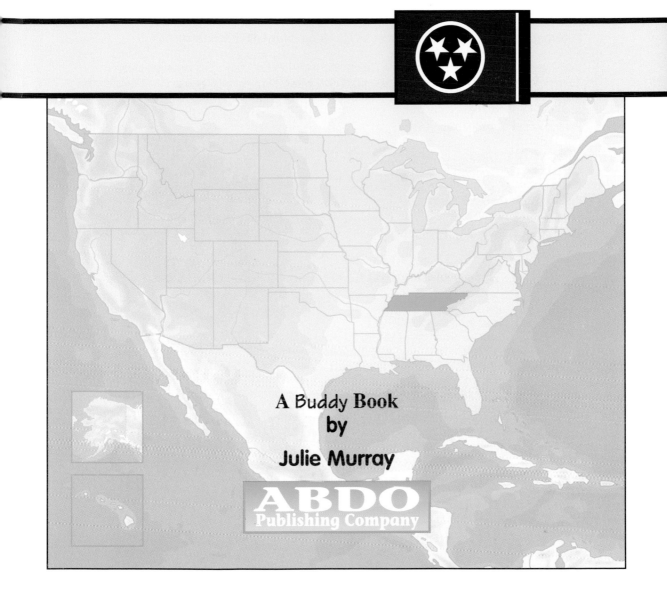

A Buddy Book
by
Julie Murray

ABDO
Publishing Company

VISIT US AT
www.abdopub.com

Published by ABDO Publishing Company, 4940 Viking Drive, Edina, Minnesota 55435.

Copyright © 2006 by Abdo Consulting Group, Inc. International copyrights reserved in all countries. No part of this book may be reproduced in any form without written permission from the publisher. Buddy Books™ is a trademark and logo of ABDO Publishing Company.

Printed in the United States.

Edited by: Sarah Tieck
Contributing Editor: Michael P. Goecke
Graphic Design: Deb Coldiron, Maria Hosley
Image Research: Sarah Tieck
Photographs: AP/Wide World, Chris Hollo, Clipart.com, Comstock, Digital Vision, Getty Images, Library of Congress, Memphistravel.com, One Mile Up, Photodisc, Photos.com, Tennessee.gov

Library of Congress Cataloging-in-Publication Data

Murray, Julie, 1969-
    Tennessee / Julie Murray.
        p. cm. — (The United States)
    ISBN 1-59197-701-0
        1. Tennessee—Juvenile literature. I. Title.

F436.3.M87 2005
976.8—dc22
                                                    2005049024

Table Of Contents

A Snapshot Of Tennessee

When people think of Tennessee, they think of music. Many people go to Nashville to become country music singers. Also, Elvis Presley lived in Memphis. He was known as the "King of Rock and Roll."

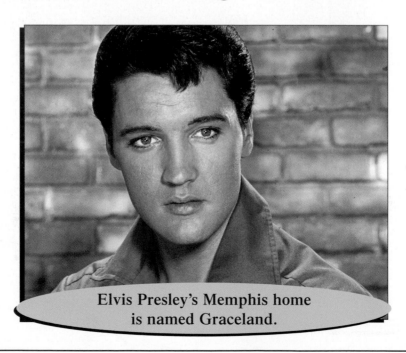

Elvis Presley's Memphis home is named Graceland.

There are 50 states in the United States. Every state is different. Every state has an official nickname. Tennessee is known as "The Volunteer State." Many volunteers from Tennessee fought in the War of 1812. This is how the state got its nickname.

Nashville is one city in Tennessee. Many people live in Tennessee's cities.

Tennessee became the 16th state on June 1, 1796. Today, it is the 34th-largest state in the United States. Tennessee has 42,146 square miles (109,158 sq km) of land. It is home to 5,689,283 people.

Tennessee is also known for its mountains.

Where Is Tennessee?

There are four parts of the United States. Each part is called a region. Each region is in a different area of the country. The United States Census Bureau says the four regions are the Northeast, the South, the Midwest, and the West.

Tennessee is located in the South region of the United States. The weather there is often warm and humid.

Four Regions of the United States of America

ALASKA

WASHINGTON
MONTANA
NORTH DAKOTA
MINNESOTA
WISCONSIN
VERMONT
MAINE
OREGON
IDAHO
WYOMING
SOUTH DAKOTA
MICHIGAN
NEW HAMPSHIRE
MASSACHUSETTS
NEW YORK
NEVADA
UTAH
COLORADO
NEBRASKA
IOWA
ILLINOIS
INDIANA
OHIO
PENNSYLVANIA
RHODE ISLAND
CONNECTICUT
NEW JERSEY
DELAWARE
Washington D.C.
MARYLAND
CALIFORNIA
ARIZONA
NEW MEXICO
KANSAS
MISSOURI
KENTUCKY
WEST VIRGINIA
VIRGINIA
NORTH CAROLINA
OKLAHOMA
ARKANSAS
TENNESSEE
SOUTH CAROLINA
MISSISSIPPI
ALABAMA
GEORGIA
TEXAS
LOUISIANA
FLORIDA

HAWAII

West

Midwest

South

Northeast

Tennessee is bordered by eight other states and America's longest river. Kentucky and Virginia are north. North Carolina is east. Georgia, Alabama, and Mississippi are south. Arkansas and Missouri are west. The Mississippi River is part of the state's western border.

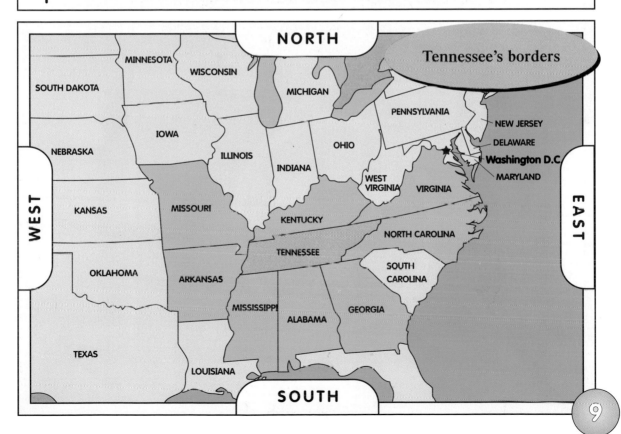

Tennessee's borders

Tennessee

State abbreviation: TN

State nickname: The Volunteer State

State capital: Nashville

State motto: Agriculture and Commerce

Statehood: June 1, 1796, 16th state

Population: 5,689,283, ranks 16th

Land area: 42,146 square miles (109,158 sq km), ranks 34th

State flag:
Adopted in 1905

State songs: "My Homeland, Tennessee," "When It's Iris Time in Tennessee," "My Tennessee," "The Tennessee Waltz," and "Rocky Top"

State government: Three branches: legislative, executive, and judicial

Average July temperature: 78°F (26°C)

Average January temperature: 38°F (3°C)

State flower:
Iris

State wild animal:
Raccoon

State bird:
Mockingbird

Cities And The Capital

Nashville is the capital city of Tennessee. It is also the second-largest city in the state. This city is located on the Cumberland River. When people think of this city, they think of country music. Nashville is home to the Grand Ole Opry and the Country Music Hall of Fame.

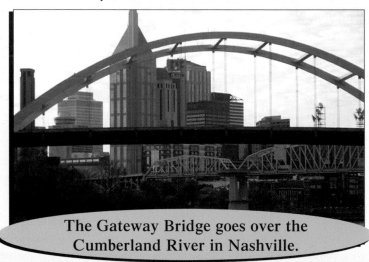

The Gateway Bridge goes over the Cumberland River in Nashville.

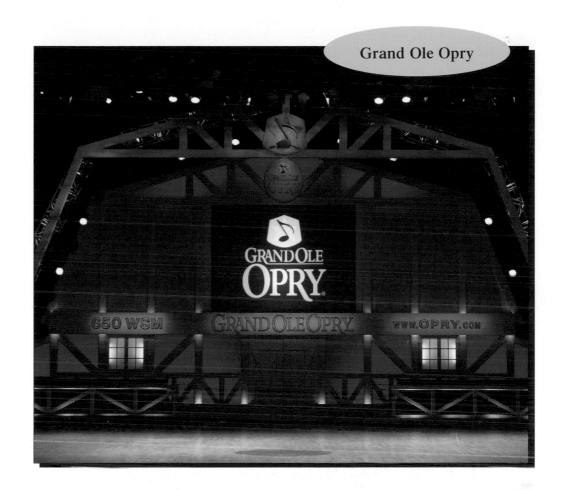

Grand Ole Opry

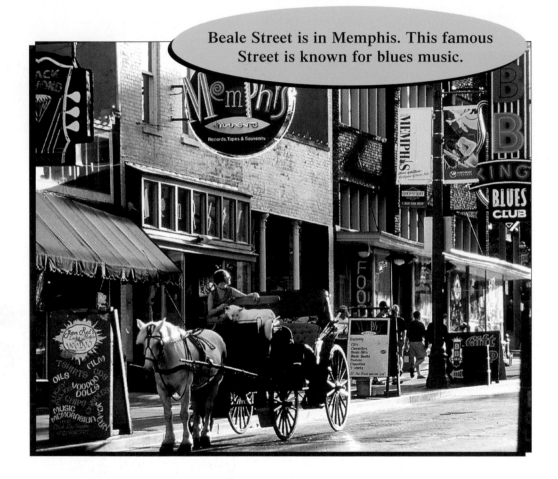

Beale Street is in Memphis. This famous Street is known for blues music.

Memphis is the largest city in Tennessee. It is on the Mississippi River, in the southwestern part of the state.

Memphis is home to a famous house called Graceland. This is where Elvis Presley lived. He is famous for singing rock-and-roll music.

The Music Gate is the entrance to Graceland.

Famous Citizens

Davy Crockett (1786–1836)

Davy Crockett was born in Greene County in 1786. He was famous for his wild stories and for being a pioneer. Crockett was also a politician. He was killed in Texas in 1836. He was there helping to fight for Texas' independence from Mexico. Today, many books, television shows, and movies tell of his life.

Davy Crockett

Famous Citizens

Al Gore Jr. (1948–)

Al Gore Jr. was born in Washington, D.C., in 1948. At this time, his father, Al Gore Sr., was serving in Congress for Tennessee. Al Gore Jr. was a politician, as well. He also represented Tennessee in Congress. In 1993, he became vice president of the United States. He served with President Bill Clinton. He ran for president against George W. Bush in 2000, but lost one of the closest elections in American History.

Al Gore Jr.

Famous Citizens

Aretha Franklin (1942–)

Aretha Franklin was born in Memphis in 1942. She is a famous singer. Some people call her the "Queen of Soul." One of her most famous songs is "Respect." She also sang "I Say a Little Prayer," "Chain of Fools," and "Lady Soul."

Aretha Franklin

Appalachian Mountains

The Appalachian Mountains run through eastern Tennessee. They form the second-largest mountain range in North America. They stretch for about 1,500 miles (2,414 km) from Quebec, Canada, to Birmingham, Alabama. The only mountain range in North America that is larger is the Rocky Mountains.

In Tennessee, the Great Smoky Mountains are part of the Appalachian Mountains. They got their name because a smoky mist covers the mountaintops. The highest point in the state is there. It is Clingmans Dome, which stands 6,643 feet (2,025 m) tall.

A view of the Great Smoky Mountains.

Trail Of Tears

In the 1800s, the western part of the United States was a great wilderness. Soon, many people began moving to the United States. The Native Americans who lived in the southeast were forced to move. This included Native Americans who lived in Tennessee.

The United States Government gave them land to live on. This area was called the Indian Territory.

In 1838, the Cherokee and other Native Americans were forced to move to the Indian Territory. There, they faced hunger, disease, and cold weather. Thousands of Native Americans died during this trip. This is why the journey became known as the "Trail of Tears."

Indian Territory

Great Smoky Mountains National Park

Great Smoky Mountains National Park is along the border of Tennessee and North Carolina. The park covers more than 800 square miles (2,072 sq km) of land.

Great Smoky Mountains National Park

There are many trees in the
Great Smoky Mountains.

Great Smoky Mountains National Park is one of the most popular national parks in the United States. More than 9 million people visit the park each year. They bike, fish, camp, and ride horses there. Also, there are many miles of hiking trails.

Cades Cove is a famous part of the park. It is located near Townsend. It has 6,800 acres (2,752 ha) of land. People come to see the scenery and wildlife. They also come to learn about the area's history and culture. People often visit the old buildings and historic settlers' homes.

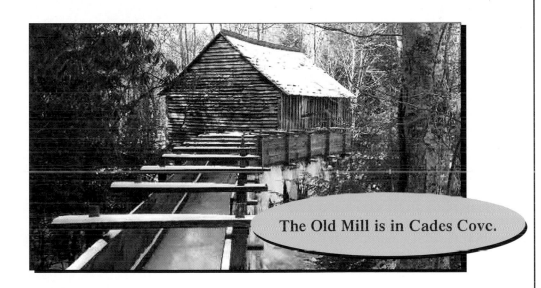

The Old Mill is in Cades Cove.

Tennessee

1540: Spanish explorer Hernando de Soto arrives in Tennessee.

1673: English explorers arrive in the Tennessee River Valley.

1775: Daniel Boone establishes the Wilderness Trail. This trail passes through the Cumberland Gap.

1796: Tennessee becomes the 16th state on June 1.

1838: Native Americans walk the Trail of Tears to the Indian Territory.

1968: Civil rights leader Martin Luther King Jr. is shot and killed in Memphis.

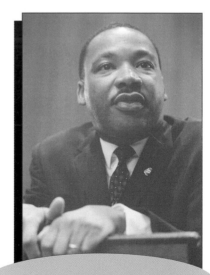

Martin Luther King Jr.

1982: Knoxville hosts the World's Fair.

1993: Al Gore Jr. becomes vice president of the United States.

1996: Tennessee celebrates its bicentennial.

Former president Bill Clinton (left) with former vice president Al Gore.

2005: Grand Ole Opry celebrates its 80th birthday. This makes it the world's longest-running radio show playing country music.

Cities In Tennessee

★ Nashville

● Knoxville

● Townsend

● Memphis

Important Words

bicentennial a 200-year anniversary.

capital a city where government leaders meet.

civil rights rights for all citizens.

humid air that is damp or moist.

nickname a name that describes something special about a person or a place.

pioneers people who traveled across the United States in the 1800s to settle the western United States.

wilderness wild, unsettled land.

Web Sites

Index